The Book of
New England Wisdom

The Book of
New England Wisdom

Common Sense and Uncommon Genius
From 101 Great New Englanders

Compiled and Edited by Criswell Freeman

WALNUT GROVE PRESS
Nashville, TN
(615) 256-8584

ISBN 1-887655-15-8

The ideas expressed in this book are not, in all cases, exact quotations, as some have been edited for clarity and brevity. In all cases, the author has attempted to maintain the speaker's original intent. In some cases, material for this book was obtained from secondary sources, primarily print media. While every effort was made to ensure the accuracy of these sources, the accuracy cannot be guaranteed. For additions, deletions, corrections or clarifications in future editions of this text, please write WALNUT GROVE PRESS.

Printed in the United States of America
Cover Design by Mary Mazer
Typesetting & Page Layout by Sue Gerdes
Edited by Alan Ross and Angela Beasley
1 2 3 4 5 6 7 8 9 10 • 96 97 98

ACKNOWLEDGMENTS
The author gratefully acknowledges the helpful support of Angela Beasley, Dick and Mary Freeman, and Mary Susan Freeman.

Table of Contents

Introduction

To fully understand the genius of America, one must first understand the genius of New England. It is the birthplace of American education and the bedrock of American philosophy. New England is a sanctuary of quiet beauty; simultaneously, it can be a rugged place where nature tests the mettle of the human spirit.

New England, like a patchwork quilt, is made up of many bits and pieces. It is as big as Boston, as peaceful as Cape Cod, as quaint as Martha's Vineyard, as historic as Bunker Hill. It is the home of Emerson and Thoreau, of Emily Dickinson and Paul Revere. It produced loquacious Jack Kennedy and silent Cal Coolidge. Its history tells a story of great thinkers, great leaders, and great educators.

This book records the wisdom of 101 noteworthy New Englanders. Among its contributors are writers, statesmen, jurists, clerics, patriots, entertainers, and teachers. Through selected quotations, these thoughtful men and women weave a philosophy of courage, determination, humor and hope. Their message is profound yet practical. More importantly, it is a message that is worthy of New England; it is the timeless wisdom of good old-fashioned Yankee common sense.

1

New England

Four centuries have passed since John Smith gave New England its name. Smith wrote, "Of all the four parts of the world that I have seen not inhabited . . . I would rather live here than anywhere." Smith was not alone.

Some came in search of profit, others in search of freedom. From the beginning, these pioneers demonstrated a gritty perseverance borne out of hardship. The tough, self-reliant Yankee became a model for the rest — and the best — of America.

The following quotations describe this land of lakes, woods, mountains, shorelines, hamlets and cities. Because of its rich diversity, no single description is sufficient. Still, this much is certain: John Smith was right. New England is a very special place.

New England is the first American section
to be finished, to achieve stability in the
conditions of its life. It is the first
old civilization, the first permanent
civilization in America.

Bernard De Voto

In Vermont, we have no populous towns,
seaports or factories to collect people
together. They are spread over the
whole country, forming small
and separate settlements.

Samuel Williams, 1794

New England is a legitimate child
of Old England, although in its minority
it became undutiful and broke
the bonds of parental restraint.

Calvin Colton

The swaggering underemphasis
of New England.

Heywood Broun

New Hampshire is
one of the two best
states in the union.
Vermont's the other.

Robert Frost

You do not know what beauty is
    if you have not been to Hartford.

Mark Twain

Nantucket!
Take out your map and look at it — a mere
   hillock, an elbow of sand — all beach,
      without a background.

Herman Melville

I believe no one attempts to praise
the climate of New England.

Harriet Martineau

If you don't like the weather in New England,
just wait a few minutes.

Ring Lardner

There is no cure for Vermont weather.
It is consistent only in its inconsistency.

Noel Perrin

Only Bostonians
can understand Bostonians.

Henry Adams

Boston is a state of mind.

Mark Twain

Boston is The Hub of the Universe.

Oliver Wendell Holmes, Sr.

The Bostonian who leaves Boston
ought to be condemned to perpetual exile.

William Dean Howells

The love of learning, learning how to learn —
was revealed to me in Boston.

Leonard Bernstein

I played before the greatest fans in baseball,
the Boston fans.

Ted Williams

Nobody can live in the Boston climate
without considerable resources.

C. F. Adams

The most serious charge
which can be brought
against New England
is not Puritanism,
but February.

Joseph Ward Krutch

2

The People

Frontiersman Davy Crockett visited New England and was thoroughly impressed by her people. In writing back to his new Yankee friends, Crockett noted, "It is your habits, and manners, and customs; your industry; your proud independent spirits; your hanging on to eternal principles of right and wrong; your liberality in prosperity and your patience when you are ground down by legislation . . . These are things that make me think you are a mighty good people."

Crockett's observations, made almost two centuries ago, still apply. Thankfully, when it comes to old-fashioned values, New Englanders are slow to change.

The prosperity of my native land,
New England, which is sterile and
unproductive, must depend hereafter
on the moral qualities and secondly,
on the intelligence and information
of the inhabitants.

John Lowell, Jr.

The Yankee: In acuteness and perseverance,
he resembles the Scotch. In frugal neatness,
he resembles the Dutch. But in truth,
a Yankee is like nothing else on earth
but himself.

Frances Trollope

Yankees see further ahead than most folks.

T. C. Haliburton

You can always tell
a Yankee, but you
can't tell him much.

Eric Knight

I love Vermont most of all
because of her indomitable people.
Calvin Coolidge

Up in the mountains of New Hampshire,
God Almighty has hung out a sign to show
that there He makes men.
Daniel Webster

Rhode Island was settled and made up
of people who found it unbearable to live
anywhere else in New England.
Woodrow Wilson

Here's to the state of Maine,
　　the land of the bluest skies, the greenest
　　earth, the richest air, the sturdiest men,
　　the fairest, and what is best, truest women
　　　　　　under the sun.

Thomas Brackett Reed

The state of Massachusetts is made up
　　of the enterprise of its inhabitants.

C. F. Adams

The People

What we meant in going after those Redcoats
was this: We always had governed ourselves,
and we always meant to.

Captain Preston

These are the times that try men's souls.

Thomas Paine

I must study politics and war
so that my sons may have liberty to study
mathematics and philosophy.

John Adams

I demand the surrender of Fort Ticonderoga
in the name of the great Jehovah and
the Continental Congress.

Ethan Allen

We fight, get beat, rise, and fight again.

General Nathanael Greene

Military power will never awe a sensible
American to surrender tamely his liberty.

Samuel Adams

There, I guess King George
will be able to read that.

John Hancock
on signing The Declaration of Independence

Stand your ground.
Don't fire unless fired upon, but if they
mean to have a war, let it begin here.

Colonel John Parker
at Lexington Green

Don't fire until you see
the whites of their eyes.

Colonel William Prescott
at the battle of Bunker Hill

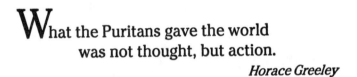

What the Puritans gave the world
was not thought, but action.

Horace Greeley

'Tis a gift to be simple.

From a Traditional Shaker Hymn

3

Character and Courage

The Roman comic poet Terence correctly observed, "Nothing is more valuable to a man than courage." Though he never made the trip, Terence would have enjoyed New England. Here, courage and character are as much a part of the scenery as the fall colors.

Native son John Kennedy faced death in World War II but looked back upon his exploits with typical Yankee understatement. "It was easy to become a hero," Kennedy observed. "They sank my boat."

Terence, I'd like you to meet Jack Kennedy . . .

The first thing is character.

J. P. Morgan

Only those who dare to fail miserably
can achieve greatly.

Robert Kennedy

Do every day something for no other reason
than that you would rather not do it, so that
when the hour of dire need draws nigh,
it may find you not unnerved
and untrained to stand the test.

William James

They conquer who believe they can.
He has not learned the first lesson of life
who does not every day surmount fear.

Ralph Waldo Emerson

Know how sublime a thing
it is to suffer and be strong.

Henry Wadsworth Longfellow

Fear always springs from ignorance.

Ralph Waldo Emerson

Fear tastes like a rusty knife,
and do not let her into your house.

John Cheever

When you get into a tight place, and it
seems you can't go on, hold on, for that's just
the place and time that the tide will turn.

Harriet Beecher Stowe

Freedom lies in being bold.

Robert Frost

Character is much easier kept
than recovered.

Thomas Paine

Choose a self and stand by it.

William James

For an impenetrable shield,
stand inside yourself.

Henry David Thoreau

The essence of greatness
is the perception that virtue is enough.

Ralph Waldo Emerson

He is rich according to what he is,
        not what he has.
Henry Ward Beecher

Sin has many tools,
    but a lie is the handle that fits them all.
Oliver Wendell Holmes, Sr.

One man, on God's side, is a majority.
Wendell Phillips

One, with God, is always a majority,
but many a martyr has been burned at the
stake while the votes were being counted.
Thomas Brackett Reed

The rule of duty and the law of joy
seem to me as one.

Oliver Wendell Holmes, Jr.

Without discipline, there is no life at all.

Katharine Hepburn

We shall hardly notice in a year or two.
You can get accustomed to anything.

Edna St. Vincent Millay

Sow an action and you reap a habit.
Sow a habit and you reap a character.
Sow a character and you reap a destiny.

William James

Pray not for safety from danger,
    but for deliverance from fear.

Ralph Waldo Emerson

Think of your forefathers.
    Think of your posterity.

John Quincy Adams

Let us never negotiate out of fear.
    But let us never fear to negotiate.

John F. Kennedy

Character is built on the debris
of our despair.

Ralph Waldo Emerson

Do the thing you fear,
and the death of fear is certain.

Ralph Waldo Emerson

The difference between perseverance
and obstinacy is that one comes
from a strong will, and the other
from a strong won't.

Henry Ward Beecher

4

The Spirit

The spirit of New England combines several themes. New Englanders appreciate the dignity of hard work. They prize their freedom, and they staunchly guard their independence. Simplicity is another treasured virtue.

In typical Yankee style, Katharine Hepburn summed up the New England spirit with a few simple words. "Genius," Hepburn observed, "is an infinite capacity for taking life by the scruff of the neck." Now that's the spirit!

All men are born free and equal,
and have certain natural, essential,
unalienable rights.

John Adams

Restriction of free thought and free speech
is the most dangerous of subversions.

William O. Douglas

Repression is the seed of revolution.

Daniel Webster

The best road to progress is freedom's road.

John F. Kennedy

He who has confidence in himself
will lead the rest.

Horace Bushnell

Distrust people who know too much about
what God wants them to do to their fellows.

Susan B. Anthony

I shall die, but that is all I will do for death.
I am not on death's payroll.

Edna St. Vincent Millay

The man is richest
whose pleasures are cheapest.
Henry David Thoreau

There is no dignity quite so impressive,
and no independence quite so important,
as living within your means.
Calvin Coolidge

Let your affairs be as two or three
and not a thousand; and keep your accounts
on a thumbnail.
Henry David Thoreau

Money often costs too much.

Ralph Waldo Emerson

Wisdom lies in taking everything with
good humor and a grain of salt.

George Santayana

To be simple is to be great.

Ralph Waldo Emerson

Some people have nothing to say
and keep on saying it.

Robert Frost

Nothing I never said
ever did me any harm.

Calvin Coolidge

The reason worry kills more people
than work is that more people
worry than work.

Robert Frost

Nothing in the world can take
the place of persistence. Talent will not.
Genius will not. Education will not.
Persistence and determination
alone are omnipotent.

Calvin Coolidge

If you don't paddle
your own canoe,
you don't move.

Katharine Hepburn

5

All-Purpose Advice

Giving advice is a very tricky business. If one gives it too freely, the advice is ignored. But if it is withheld altogether, people may suffer needlessly.

What is the solution? The answer is found in the book of Proverbs, where it is written, "In the multitude of counselors, there is safety."

The following words of wisdom come from a multitude of sage New England advisors. Heed them . . . for safety's sake.

Once a decision is reached,
stop worrying and start working.

William James

Look not mournfully into the past.
It comes not back again. Wisely improve
the present. It is thine. Go forth to meet
the shadowy future, without fear.

Henry Wadsworth Longfellow

Mind you own business, do no wrong,
sleep your siesta when necessary,
and trust in God.

John Adams

His advice to Thomas Jefferson

We must be careful what we say. No bird resumes its egg.

Emily Dickinson

See the miraculous in the commonplace.
Henry David Thoreau

Our life is frittered away by detail . . .
Simplify, simplify.
Henry David Thoreau

Read the best books first.
Henry David Thoreau

Adopt the pace of nature;
    her secret is patience.
                    Ralph Waldo Emerson

Nature is always hinting at us.
                    Robert Frost

Nature speaks in symbols and signs.
                    John Greenleaf Whittier

Don't talk unless
    you can improve the silence.
                    New England Saying

If you don't say anything,
    you won't be called upon to repeat it.
                    Calvin Coolidge

Be patient, take the bad with the good,
and never look back.
Tom Yawkey

Live each day as it comes and do not borrow
trouble from tomorrow. It is the dark menace
of the future that makes cowards of us all.
Dorothea Dix

Never do anything you should be afraid
to do if it were the last hour of your life.
Jonathan Edwards

Give me a person who says,
"This is the one thing I do," and not,
"These fifty things I dabble in."

Dwight L. Moody

You are young and have the world
before you. Stoop as you go through it
and you will miss many hard bumps.

Cotton Mather

Advice to Ben Franklin as Franklin approached
a low beam in Mather's parsonage

Only a fool holds out for the top dollar.

Joseph P. Kennedy

Goodwill is the one and only asset
that competition cannot undersell or destroy.

Marshall Field

No one can wear one face to himself and
another to the multitude without
finally wondering which is true.

Nathaniel Hawthorne

Beware of over-great pleasure
in being popular.

Margaret Fuller

Put not your trust in money,
but put your money in trust.

Oliver Wendell Holmes, Sr.

It's no good arguing with the inevitable.

James Russell Lowell

When a dog runs at you,
              whistle for him.

Henry David Thoreau

The time to repair the roof
        is when the sun is shining.

John F. Kennedy

Look up and not down.
Look forward
and not back.
Look out and not in,
and lend a hand.

Edward Everett Hale

6

Work

New Englanders appreciate the dignity of a hard day's work and the value of craftsmanship. There's an old Maine saying, "A job started right is a job half done." The following thoughts come courtesy of men and women who have started — and finished — many jobs. And they've passed along the belief that any job worth doing is worth doing well.

Yankee craftsmanship is no accident. That's just the way work is done in New England.

D̲o the day's work.

Calvin Coolidge

E̲very man is a consumer
and ought to be a producer.

Ralph Waldo Emerson

Y̲ou cannot kill time
without injury to eternity.

Henry David Thoreau

T̲he reward of a thing well done
is to have done it.

Ralph Waldo Emerson

T̲he world is full of willing people — some
willing to work, the rest willing to let them.

Robert Frost

Work is not a curse.
It is the prerogative
of the intelligent.

Calvin Coolidge

The notion that work is a burden
is a terrible mistake. Working and
facing up to one's responsibilities:
That's happiness.

Katharine Hepburn

You have freedom
when you're easy in your harness.

Robert Frost

Perseverance can do anything
which genius can do, and very many things
which genius cannot.

Henry Ward Beecher

Ideas must work through the brains
and the arms of good and brave men,
or they are no better than dreams.

Ralph Waldo Emerson

Let us go forth, asking His blessing
and His help, but knowing that here on earth,
God's work must truly be our own.

John F. Kennedy

Let us then be up and doing with a heart
for any fate. Still achieving, still pursuing,
learn to labor and to wait.

Henry Wadsworth Longfellow

Run, if you like, but try to keep your breath.
Work like a man, but don't be worked to death.

Oliver Wendell Holmes, Sr.

If you believe in the Lord, He will do half the work: the last half.

Cyrus Curtis

7

Happiness

In his play *Antigone*, Sophocles observes, "Our happiness depends on wisdom all the way." Thus, we turn to wise New Englanders for a few lessons about the subject of happiness.

Rhode Islanders have a saying: "Happiness is like jam. You can't spread it around without getting a little on yourself." On the following pages we share quotations about wisdom and joy. Consider the message — then spread it around.

Happiness lies, first of all, in health.
George William Curtis

Happiness is a butterfly,
which when pursued, is always just beyond
your grasp, but which if you sit down quietly,
may alight upon you.
Nathaniel Hawthorne

To fill the now — that is happiness;
to fill the now and leave no device
for a repentance or an approval.
Ralph Waldo Emerson

Happiness, to some elation,
is to others, mere stagnation.
Amy Lowell

Happiness is a perfume
you can't pour on others without getting
a few drops on yourself.

Ralph Waldo Emerson

Happiness makes up in height for
what it lacks in length.

Robert Frost

Humor makes all things tolerable.

Henry Ward Beecher

There is no more miserable human being
than one in whom nothing is habitual
but indecision.

William James

Discontent is want of self-reliance.

Ralph Waldo Emerson

Nothing is so fatiguing as the hanging on
of an uncompleted task.

William James

Don't craze yourself with too much thinking.
Just go about your business.

Ralph Waldo Emerson

If you always do what interests you, at least one person is pleased.

Mother's Advice to Katharine Hepburn

Five great enemies of peace inhabit us:
avarice, ambition, envy, anger and pride.
Ralph Waldo Emerson

Many of our disappointments
and much of our unhappiness arise from our
forming false notions of things and persons.
Abigail Adams

Most of the shadows of this life are caused
by standing on one's own sunshine.
Ralph Waldo Emerson

Happiness is not the end of life —
character is.

Henry Ward Beecher

The mere sense of living is joy enough.

Emily Dickinson

Man is the artificer of his own happiness.

Henry David Thoreau

The happiest man is he who learns
from nature the lesson of worship.
Ralph Waldo Emerson

The landscape belongs to the man
who looks at it.
Henry David Thoreau

This is the last of earth. I am content.
John Quincy Adams
His Last Words

Eden is that
old-fashioned house
we dwell in every day
without suspecting
our abode
until we drive away.

Emily Dickinson

When the Red Sox win, all of New England feels great.

Vin Scully

8

Love and Friendship

New England is a place where people are not afraid to put down roots. Several generations may live in the same small town. Friendships span lifetimes. For many, New England remains an island of continuity in a world of change.

We examine the topics of friendship and love through the words of men and women who have known both — New England style.

The best servant does his work unseen.
Oliver Wendell Holmes, Sr.

Every man should have
a fair-sized cemetery in which to bury
the faults of his friends.
Henry Ward Beecher

Look upon the errors of others in sorrow,
not in anger.
Henry Wadsworth Longfellow

Behind every argument
is someone's ignorance.
Louis Brandeis

The only way
to have a friend
is to be one.

Ralph Waldo Emerson

The deepest principle
of human nature
is the craving
to be appreciated.

William James

A friend may well be reckoned
the masterpiece of nature.
Ralph Waldo Emerson

Real unselfishness consists
in sharing the interests of others.
George Santayana

You never know until you try to reach them
how accessible men are; but you must
approach each man by the right door.
Henry Ward Beecher

In life, you can never do a kindness
too soon because you never know
how soon it will be too late.
Ralph Waldo Emerson

Love . . . the essence of God.

Ralph Waldo Emerson

Till it has loved, no man or woman
can become itself.

Emily Dickinson

Love is not enough.
It must be the foundation, the cornerstone,
but not the complete structure. It is much
too pliable, too yielding.

Bette Davis

The only gift is a portion of thyself.

Ralph Waldo Emerson

Give what you have. To someone,
it may be better than you dare think.

Henry Wadsworth Longfellow

Nothing dies so hard, or rallies so often,
as intolerance.

Henry Ward Beecher

A cynic can chill and dishearten
with a single word.

Ralph Waldo Emerson

"I can forgive, but I cannot forget,"
is only another way of saying,
"I will not forgive."

Henry Ward Beecher

Whatever you may be sure of,
be sure of this: You are
dreadfully like other people.

James Russell Lowell

Folks never understand the folks they hate.

James Russell Lowell

No man is more cheated
than the selfish man.

Henry Ward Beecher

What is lovely never dies
but passes into
other loveliness.

Thomas Bailey Aldrich

9

Action

New Englanders don't believe in letting a problem fester. As the patriot Josiah Quincy observed, "When you have a number of disagreeable duties to perform, always do the most disagreeable first."

The beloved poet Robert Frost was born in San Francisco and did not move East until he was a young man. Thus, it can be said he remained a New Englander by choice. Frost once noted, "The best way out is always through." With these words, he displayed an authentic Yankee bias for action.

Do not delay; the golden moments fly.
Henry Wadsworth Longfellow

We have too many high sounding words,
and too few actions to go with them.
Abigail Adams

As a man thinketh so is he,
and as a man chooseth, so is he.
Ralph Waldo Emerson

All the beautiful sentiments in the world
weigh less than a single lovely action.
James Russell Lowell

Seize the first opportunity
to act on every resolution
you make.

William James

B̲e willing to commit yourself to a course,
perhaps a long and hard one,
without being able to foresee exactly
where you will come out.
Oliver Wendell Holmes, Jr.

D̲eeds are better things than words are.
Actions are mightier than boastings.
Henry Wadsworth Longfellow

E̲fforts and courage are not enough
without purpose and direction.
John F. Kennedy

A̲ man's action
is only a picture book of his creed.
Ralph Waldo Emerson

We cannot do everything at once, but we can do something at once.

Calvin Coolidge

Life is action and passion.

Oliver Wendell Holmes, Jr.

The bitterest tears shed over graves
are for words left unsaid and
deeds left undone.

Harriet Beecher Stowe

When you have a choice and don't make it,
that is in itself a choice.

William James

It is not enough to be busy.
The question is what are we busy about.

Henry David Thoreau

Liberty is the power to do things.

John Dewey

Habit is stronger than reason.

George Santayana

There is no shortcut to fame and comfort.
You simply bore into it
as hard as you can.

Oliver Wendell Holmes, Jr.

Men have never fully used their powers
because they have waited upon some power
external to themselves to do the work
they are responsible for doing.

John Dewey

What I need most is somebody
to make me do what I can.

Ralph Waldo Emerson

Not failure, but low aim, is the crime.

James Russell Lowell

For of all sad words
of tongue or pen,
The saddest are these:
"It might have been!"

John Greenleaf Whittier

Lift where you stand.

Edward Everett Hale

10

Attitude

Ralph Waldo Emerson, the "Sage of Concord," was nothing if not an optimist. He believed each of us is gifted with a quiet, inner compass which is available whenever we muster the curiosity and courage to look inward for guidance. An integral part of this inner journey depends upon one's attitude toward life.

As Emerson correctly observed, "A man is what he thinks about all day long." If one looks for the best, one finds it. If one seeks the worst, this becomes reality.

The following pages document New Englanders' attitudes about attitude. As you read these words, consider this sobering truth: The world in which you live must, over time, fit into the mold of your own expectations.

Alter your life by altering your attitudes.

William James

Mirth is God's medicine.
Everybody ought to bathe in it.

Henry Ward Beecher

Happiness in this world, if it comes at all,
comes incidentally. Make it the object
of pursuit, and it leads us on a wild-goose
chase and is never attained.

Nathaniel Hawthorne

Write on your heart that every day
is the best day of the year.

Ralph Waldo Emerson

What is required is sight and insight – then you might add one more: excite.

Robert Frost

They can conquer who believe they can.

Ralph Waldo Emerson

Every great and commanding moment
in the annals of history is a triumph
of someone's enthusiasm.

Ralph Waldo Emerson

Nothing great was ever achieved
without enthusiasm.

Ralph Waldo Emerson

Never take away hope
from any human being.

Oliver Wendell Holmes, Sr.

Hope is a thing with feathers,
      that perches on the soul.

Emily Dickinson

The reason for idleness and crime
      is the deferring of our hopes.

Ralph Waldo Emerson

Entertain great hopes.

Robert Frost

In any project, the important factor
is your belief. Without belief there
can be no successful outcome.

William James

Every tomorrow has two handles:
We can take hold of the handle of anxiety
or the handle of faith.

Henry Ward Beecher

To me, faith is not worrying.

John Dewey

The fault-finder will find faults even in paradise.

Henry David Thoreau

Never bear more than one trouble at a time.
Some people bear three kinds:
all they have had, all they have now,
and all they expect to have.

Edward Everett Hale

Don't be a cynic and bewail and bemoan.
Omit the negative propositions.
Don't waste yourself in reflection,
nor bark against the bad, but
chant the beauty of the good.

Ralph Waldo Emerson

To be ignorant of one's ignorance
is the malady of the ignorant.

Bronson Alcott

Nothing can bring you peace
but yourself.

Ralph Waldo Emerson

Poverty consists in feeling poor.

Ralph Waldo Emerson

Calmness is always Godlike.

Ralph Waldo Emerson

Keep cool.
It will all be over 100 years hence.

Ralph Waldo Emerson

Though we travel
the world over to find
the beautiful, we must
carry it with us,
or we find it not.

Ralph Waldo Emerson

Love is a great beautifier.

Louisa May Alcott

11

Adversity

New England is blessed with great natural beauty, but it can be a hard place to scratch out a living. The weather is sometimes daunting, and the work is sometimes hard. What's required is a certain brand of Yankee toughness. That's why New Englanders have little patience with chronic bellyaching.

Steven Vincent Benét once responded to an unreasonable complaint with the following words: "As for what you're calling bad luck — well, we made New England out of it. That and codfish."

If you're facing adversity, contemplate the words that follow. Then fashion something beautiful out of your misfortune.

Every calamity is a spur and valuable hint.

Ralph Waldo Emerson

Every sweet hath its sour,
  every evil its good.

Ralph Waldo Emerson

It is defeat which educates us.

Ralph Waldo Emerson

One thorn of experience is worth
a whole wilderness of warning.

James Russell Lowell

Make the most of your regrets.

Henry David Thoreau

Men's best successes come
after their disappointments.

Henry Ward Beecher

The nearer the dawn, the darker the night.

Henry Wadsworth Longfellow

Into each life some rain must fall.
Some days must be dark and dreary.
Henry Wadsworth Longfellow

Difficulties exist to be surmounted.
Ralph Waldo Emerson

Troubles are often the tools by which
God fashions us for better things.
Henry Ward Beecher

All experience is an arch, to build upon.
Henry Adams

The lowest ebb is the turn of the tide.
Henry Wadsworth Longfellow

Birds sing after a storm.
Why shouldn't we?

Rose Fitzgerald Kennedy

The misfortunes hardest to bear are
those that never come.

James Russell Lowell

Acceptance is the first step
to overcoming any misfortune.

William James

Many of our troubles are God dragging us,
and they would end if we would stand upon
our feet and go whither He would have us go.

Henry Ward Beecher

From those who have never sailed come
the quickest and harshest judgments
on bad seamanship.

Susan Glaspell

When one door closes, another opens,
but we often look so long and so regretfully
upon the closed door that we do not see
the one which has opened for us.

Alexander Graham Bell

Finish every day and be done with it.
You have done what you could.
Some blunders and absurdities
no doubt have crept in;
forget them as soon as you can.

Ralph Waldo Emerson

The best thing one can do when it's raining is let it rain.

Henry Wadsworth Longfellow

<u>12</u>

Life

Two thousand years ago, Marcus Aurelius warned, "Do not act as if you had a thousand years to live." The Roman philosopher-king understood that our days on earth are too few to be spent carelessly. But each human being faces a personal dilemma: how to use a life wisely. Kierkegaard recognized the predicament when he observed, "Life can only be understood backward, but it must be lived forward."

To further confound matters, life's greatest challenges are seldom, if ever, solved "once and for all." Edna St. Vincent Millay wrote, "It's not that life is one darn thing after another. It's one darn thing over and over."

On these pages, wise New Englanders help you reflect on birth, death, and what to do in between.

The cost of a thing is the amount of life
that must be exchanged for it.

Henry David Thoreau

The Indian summer of life should be
a little sunny and a little sad, like the season,
and infinite in wealth and depth of tone —
but never hustled.

Henry Adams

All life is an experiment.
The more experiments you make the better.

Ralph Waldo Emerson

Live all you can. It's a mistake not to.

Henry James

Life is a series of lessons
that must be lived to be understood.

Ralph Waldo Emerson

Believe that life is worth living and your belief will help create the fact.

William James

Life is a great bundle of little things.
Oliver Wendell Holmes, Sr.

Life is painting a picture, not doing a sum.
Oliver Wendell Holmes, Jr.

That it will never come again
is what makes life so sweet.
Emily Dickinson

Who loses a day loses a life.
Ralph Waldo Emerson

You are only sure of today;
do not let yourself be cheated out of it.
Henry Ward Beecher

Death tugs at my ear and says,
"Live, I am coming."

Oliver Wendell Holmes, Sr.

Man is unjust, but God is just;
and finally justice triumphs.

Henry Wadsworth Longfellow

Every man's life is a plan of God.

Horace Bushnell

It is only when men begin to worship
that they begin to grow.

Calvin Coolidge

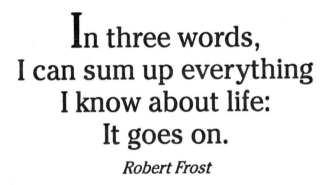

In three words,
I can sum up everything
I know about life:
It goes on.

Robert Frost

13

Success

Henry David Thoreau, in his wisdom, understood that success comes in many different shapes and sizes. He wrote, "If a man does not keep pace with his companions, perhaps it is because he hears a different drummer. Let him step to the music he hears, however measured or far away."

A century after Thoreau wrote these words, America welcomed a newcomer who truly marched to the beat of his own drum: Albert Einstein. Einstein warned, "Try not to be a man of success, but rather try to be a man of value." The Swiss physicist understood a simple yet profound truth: Without values, success is impossible; but with values, success is inevitable.

Self-trust is the first secret of success.
Ralph Waldo Emerson

There is always room at the top.
Daniel Webster

Act the part and you will become the part.
William James

The secret of my success is that
at an early age I discovered I was not God.
Oliver Wendell Holmes, Jr.

Be ashamed to die
until you have won some
victory for humanity.

Horace Mann

No great advance has ever been made
in science, politics or religion
without controversy.

Lyman Beecher

Fame is a fickle food
upon a shifting plate.

Emily Dickinson

Fame usually comes to those
who are thinking about something else.

Oliver Wendell Holmes, Sr.

The greatest use of a life is to spend it
for something that will outlast it.

William James

Prosperity is only an instrument to be used,
not a deity to be worshipped.

Calvin Coolidge

No man can tell whether
he is rich or poor by turning to his ledger.
It is the heart that makes a man rich.

Henry Ward Beecher

The success of any great moral enterprise
does not depend upon numbers.

William Lloyd Garrison

Success in business is his who earns
a living pursuing his highest pleasure.

Henry David Thoreau

Where we stand is not as important
as the direction in which we are moving.

Oliver Wendell Holmes, Jr.

Pursue some path,
however narrow and crooked, in which
you can walk with love and reverence.

Henry David Thoreau

It is not the going out of port,
but the coming in that determines
the success of the voyage.

Henry Ward Beecher

This time, like all times, is a very good one
if we but know what to do with it.

Ralph Waldo Emerson

Weep not that the world changes —
did it keep a stable, changeless state,
it were cause indeed to weep.

William Cullen Bryant

Don't fight forces, use them.

Buckminster Fuller

What lies behind us and what lies before us
are tiny matters compared
to what lies within us.

Ralph Waldo Emerson

Alas for those who never sing,
but die with their music still in them.
Oliver Wendell Holmes, Sr.

A grave, wherever found, preaches
a short and pithy sermon to the soul.
Nathaniel Hawthorne

Live your life, do your work,
then take your hat.
Henry David Thoreau

14

Wisdom

Born in Spain, philosopher George Santayana spent many years in New England. He once observed, "Almost every wise saying has an opposite one, no less wise, to balance it."

On the following pages, you will find an assortment of wise sayings. It's up to you to discover any counterbalancing truths.

Life is a festival only to the wise.

Ralph Waldo Emerson

Knowledge and timber shouldn't be used until they are seasoned.

Oliver Wendell Holmes, Sr.

The wisest mind has something yet to learn.

George Santayana

No one can produce great things who is not thoroughly sincere in dealing with himself.

James Russell Lowell

Search thine own heart. What paineth thee in others in thyself may be.

John Greenleaf Whittier

Those who cannot remember the past
are condemned to repeat it.

George Santayana

Liberty cannot be preserved
without education.

John Adams

In all things, the supreme excellence
is simplicity.

Henry Wadsworth Longfellow

First, master the fundamentals.

Larry Bird

The fear of ideas
    makes us impotent and ineffective.

William O. Douglas

Genius borrows nobly.

Ralph Waldo Emerson

An idea is a feat of association.

Robert Frost

Genius is little more than thinking
    in an unhabitual way.

William James

A great many people believe
they are thinking when they are merely
rearranging their prejudices.

William James

A concept is stronger than a fact.

Charlotte Perkins Gilman

A thought is often original though
you have uttered it a thousand times.

Oliver Wendell Holmes, Sr.

In every work of genius we recognize
our own rejected thoughts.

Ralph Waldo Emerson

The mind, once expanded to the dimensions
of larger ideas, never returns
to its original size.
Oliver Wendell Holmes, Jr.

If we would be guided by the light of reason,
we must let our minds be bold.
Louis Brandeis

The foolish and the dead
alone never change their opinions.
James Russell Lowell

A child educated only at school
is an undereducated child.
George Santayana

The human mind is like an umbrella – it functions best when open.

Walter Gropius

The years teach much
　　　which the days never know.
　　　　　　　Ralph Waldo Emerson

Learn by doing.
　　　　　　　John Dewey

Wisdom is the fruit of experience,
　　　not the lessons of retirement and leisure.
　　　Great necessities call out great virtues.
　　　　　　　Abigail Adams

The better part of every man's education
　　　is that which he gives himself.
　　　　　　　James Russell Lowell

We are all wise for other people,
none for himself.
Ralph Waldo Emerson

It is a characteristic of wisdom
not to do desperate things.
Henry David Thoreau

Wisdom is knowing what to overlook.
William James

It is wisdom to believe the heart.

George Santayana

15

Observations on Truth, Taxes and Other Necessities of Life

We conclude with assorted thoughts on a wide range of topics. Enjoy.

E conomy is one of the highest essentials
of a free government.

Calvin Coolidge

The greatest dangers to liberty lurk
in insidious encroachment by men of zeal,
well-meaning but without understanding.

Louis Brandeis

There is no greater inequality than
the equal treatment of unequals.

Felix Frankfurter

The power to tax is the power to destroy.

Calvin Coolidge

Collecting more taxes
than is absolutely
necessary is
legalized robbery.

Calvin Coolidge

We live under a government
of men and morning newspapers.

Wendell Phillips

To hear some men talk, you would suppose
that Congress was the law of gravitation and
kept the planets in place.

Wendell Phillips

The best use of good laws is to teach men
to trample bad laws under their feet.

Wendell Phillips

Eternal vigilance is the price of liberty.

Wendell Phillips

Any fool can make a rule.

Henry David Thoreau

The fact that talk may be
boring or uninspiring should not cause us
to forget the fact that it is preferable to war.

Henry Cabot Lodge

Civil or federal liberty is the proper end
and object of authority. It is a liberty to do
that only which is good, just and honest.

John Winthrop

Mine eyes have seen the glory of the
coming of the Lord, He is trampling out the
vintage where the grapes of wrath are stored.

Julia Ward Howe

Persecution for the cause of conscience
is most brutally contrary to
the doctrine of Christ Jesus.

Roger Williams

Controversial proposals,
once accepted, soon become hallowed.

Dean Achenson

The function of leadership is to produce
more leaders, not more followers.

Ralph Nader

Facts are stubborn things.

John Adams

Information is the currency of democracy.

Ralph Nader

Show me someone who never gossips,
and I'll show you someone who
isn't interested in people.

Barbara Walters

It is presumptuous to say that the
only thing that matters is the "bottom line."
The bottom line is in heaven.

Edwin Land

Money is
a terrible master but
an excellent servant.

P. T. Barnum

Truth is tough. It will not break.

Oliver Wendell Holmes, Sr.

Truth is as old as God.

Emily Dickinson

Good hides things
by putting them
near us.

Ralph Waldo Emerson

People only leave Washington
by way of the box: ballot or coffin.
Claiborne Pell

Before you become a statesman,
you must first be elected, and to be elected
you must first be a politician.
Margaret Chase Smith

The dangers of a concentration of all power
in the general government so vast as ours
are too obvious to be disregarded.
Franklin Pierce

All politics are local.

Tip O'Neill

The law must be stable
   but it must not stand still.
        Roscoe Pound

You have the God-given right
   to kick the government around.
    Don't hesitate to do it.
        Edmund Muskie

Charismatic leadership is hungered for —
     but feared.
        Kevin White

Revolutions never go backward.
        Wendell Phillips

If you want to know what a man
is really like, take notice how he acts
when he loses money.

New England Proverb

No great man ever complains
of want of opportunity.

Ralph Waldo Emerson

Every artist was first an amateur.

Ralph Waldo Emerson

We are always paid for our suspicions
by finding out what we expect.

Henry David Thoreau

Dare to be naive.

Buckminster Fuller

Oh, the places you'll go,
oh, the things you will see.

Dr. Seuss

Find the journey's end
in every step.

Ralph Waldo Emerson

No generalization is completely true, including this one.

Oliver Wendell Holmes, Jr.

About the Author

Criswell Freeman is a Doctor of Clinical Psychology living in Nashville, Tennessee. He is the author of *When Life Throws You a Curveball, Hit It* and *The Wisdom Series* from WALNUT GROVE PRESS. He is also a published country music songwriter.

About Wisdom Books

Wisdom Books chronicle memorable quotations in an easy-to-read style. Written by Criswell Freeman, this series provides inspiring, thoughtful and humorous messages from entertainers, athletes, scientists, politicians, clerics, writers and renegades. Each title focuses on a particular region or special interest.

Combining his passion for quotations with extensive training in psychology, Dr. Freeman revisits timeless themes such as perseverance, courage, love, forgiveness and faith.

"Quotations help us remember the simple yet profound truths that give life perspective and meaning," notes Freeman. "When it comes to life's most important lessons, we can all use gentle reminders."

The Wisdom Series
by Dr. Criswell Freeman

Wisdom Made In America
ISBN 1-887655-07-7

The Book of Southern Wisdom
ISBN 0-9640955-3-X

The Wisdom of the Midwest
ISBN 1-887655-17-4

The Book of Texas Wisdom
ISBN 0-9640955-8-0

The Book of Florida Wisdom
ISBN 0-9640955-9-9

The Book of California Wisdom
ISBN 1-887655-14-X

The Book of New England Wisdom
ISBN 1-887655-15-8

The Book of New York Wisdom
ISBN 1-887655-16-6

The Book of Country Music Wisdom
ISBN 0-9640955-1-3

The Wisdom of Old-Time Television
ISBN 1-887655-64-6

The Golfer's Book of Wisdom
ISBN 0-9640955-6-4

The Wisdom of Southern Football
ISBN 0-9640955-7-2

The Book of Stock Car Wisdom
ISBN 1-887655-12-3

The Wisdom of Old-Time Baseball
ISBN 1-887655-13-1

The Book of Football Wisdom
ISBN 1-887655-18-2

Wisdom Books are available through booksellers everywhere.
For information about a retailer near you, call 1-800-256-8584.